EPICURUS

LETTER
ON HAPPINESS

EPICURUS

LETTER
ON HAPPINESS

Translated by Robin Waterfield

CHRONICLE BOOKS

SAN FRANCISCO

First published in North America in 1994 by Chronicle Books.
Originally published in 1993 by Rider, an imprint of Ebury Press, London.
Translation copyright © 1993 by Robin Waterfield.

Jacket design by Jill Jacobson.
Book design by David Fordham.
Typeset by SX Composing Ltd., Rayleigh, Essex and
TBC Electronic Publishing, Shaftesbury, Dorset.

ISBN 0-8118-0829-7
Library of Congress Cataloging-in-Publication Data available.

Distributed in Canada by Raincoast Books
112 East Third Avenue, Vancouver, B.C. V5T 1C8

10 9 8 7 6 5 4 3 2 1

Chronicle Books
275 Fifth Street
San Francisco, California 94103

Printed and bound in Hong Kong.

CONTENTS

INTRODUCTION

A t the end of Tolstoy's novel *Anna Karenina*, Levin – an image of Tolstoy himself – understands that he 'had been happy whenever he was not thinking of the meaning of his life. What did that show? It showed that he had lived well, but thought

badly.' *Life itself, and not my reason,* he realizes, *has given me the answer about how I should live.* Levin discovers that the values implied in the way he *lived* were better than the way he *thought*, and that, if his mind could adopt them, they would enable him to 'look after his soul and remember God' and thereby reach a fuller happiness. His mind must learn how to think from the practical wisdom gained in his experience.

I f we try to finish the sentence, 'the happy person is one who . . . ', no single answer will exhaust the possible descriptions,

and what brings happiness to one person ill fits another. We cannot be too precise about what happiness is: like 'goodness' and 'integrity', to which it is connected, 'happiness' has blurred edges. We would naturally relate it to a sense of contentedness, integration, fulfilment, wholeness, even, for some, to a state of grace and blessedness. Often we reach it without aiming for it.

Like Levin, we can be happy without being able to think clearly about it, but there is always a moral side to it: a disordered life, or a life of compromised integrity, breeds discontent. Epicurus

wrote that 'a life without intelligence, decency and morality is not a pleasant life, and a life without pleasure is not an intelligent, decent and moral life.' An ordered and virtuous life is also a happy life for him. He was no Epicurean sensualist, and would have questioned Blake's aphorism that 'the road of excess leads to the palace of wisdom'. For Epicurus, 'the just person enjoys the greatest peace of mind, while the unjust is full of the utmost disquiet': to be happy, you have to live justly. Happiness is, for him, our natural condition which we can recover, guided by our instinct for pleasure and our avoidance of pain. It is, minimally and fundamentally, health of

body and tranquillity of soul, but Epicurus also thought that a life of pleasure accompanied a life of virtue.

If, for Epicurus, happiness is pleasure and the avoidance of spiritual anxiety, he is also clear about the most fruitful ingredient for a happy life: 'of all the means which are offered by wisdom to ensure happiness through the whole of life, by far the most important is having friends'. The wise person will have the same feeling for the sorrows and joys of friends as for his or her own.

With characteristic pragmatism, he suggests that there is no happiness unless we love our friends to the same degree as we love ourselves. Friendship, he says strikingly, dances round the world bidding all of us awake to our natural state of happiness.

But there are still some awkward questions about happiness, since we cannot simply will to be happy and we are always subject to necessity and chance: can everyone be happy? can we be happy all the time? can we be happy even when misfortune arises? Epicurus answers yes to these questions: it is neither too early nor

too late to seek happiness; it can be a constant feature of life; and it can endure even the most painful circumstances.

A person who chooses prison, rather than collaborate with tyranny, will, strangely, be further on the road to happiness than one who takes the easy way out. There are more significant values than personal safety and they play their part in a fulfilled life, as Epicurus acknowledges: 'though he is being tortured on the rack, the wise man is still happy'. Why? 'Because the highest pleasure lies in a serenity of soul free from fear and strong enough to

endure, as Epicurus himself did, a long illness before his death. His views, as always, are grounded in his practice of living, and, as Levin discovered, the wisdom of experience can be trusted to shape the soul.

John McDade, S. J.

 14

LETTER
ON HArPPINESS

Epicurus to Menoeceus

Ἐπίκουρος Μενοικεῖ χαίρειν

 17

μήτε νέος τις ὢν μελλέτω φιλοσοφεῖν, μήτε
γέρων ὑπάρχων κοπιάτω φιλοσοφῶν. οὔτε γὰρ
ἄωρος οὐδείς ἐστιν οὔτε πάρωρος πρὸς τὸ κατὰ
ψυχὴν ὑγιαῖνον. ὁ δὲ λέγων ἢ μήπω τοῦ
φιλοσοφεῖν ὑπάρχειν ὥραν ἢ παρεληλυθέναι τὴν
ὥραν ὅμοιός ἐστι τῷ λέγοντι πρὸς εὐδαιμονίαν
ἢ μὴ παρεῖναι τὴν ὥραν ἢ μηκέτι εἶναι. ὥστε
φιλοσοφητέον καὶ νέῳ καὶ γέροντι, τῷ μὲν ὅπως

Philosophy is essential for everyone: young people should take it up without delay, and old people should keep at it without tiring. Why? Because there's no upper or lower age limit on mental health. To say that the time for philosophy hasn't yet arrived, or that it's passed, is equivalent to telling someone, 'It's too soon – or too late – for you to be happy.' So people of all ages should practise philosophy. The advantage for a

γηράσκων νεάζῃ τοῖς ἀγαθοῖς διὰ τὴν χάριν τῶν γεγονότων, τῷ δὲ ὅπως νέος ἅμα καὶ παλαιὸς ᾖ διὰ τὴν ἀφοβίαν τῶν μελλόντων· μελετᾶν οὖν χρὴ τὰ ποιοῦντα τὴν εὐδαιμονίαν, εἴπερ παρούσης μὲν αὐτῆς πάντα ἔχομεν, ἀπούσης δὲ πάντα πράττομεν εἰς τὸ ταύτην ἔχειν.

young man is that, as he grows old, he can look back with satisfaction over his past and let the good things he has gained keep him young; the advantage for an old man is that he can be young as well as old, in the sense that he can face the future without fear. In short, we should occupy our time with things which make us happy, because happiness makes our lives complete when it's there and is the goal of all our actions when it isn't.

ἃ δέ σοι συνεχῶς παρήγγελλον, ταῦτα καὶ
πρᾶττε καὶ μελέτα, στοιχεῖα τοῦ καλῶς ζῆν
ταῦτ᾽ εἶναι διαλαμβάνων. πρῶτον μὲν τὸν θεὸν
ζῷον ἄφθαρτον καὶ μακάριον νομίζων, ὡς ἡ κοινὴ
τοῦ θεοῦ νόησις ὑπεγράφη, μηθὲν μήτε τῆς
ἀφθαρσίας ἀλλότριον μήτε τῆς μακαριότητος
ἀνοίκειον αὐτῷ πρόσαπτε· πᾶν δὲ τὸ φυλάττειν

I want you to put into wholehearted practice the teachings I've been constantly drumming into you; I want you to understand that they constitute a recipe for the good life. The most important thing is to think of God as an immortal and blessed being (which conforms with the common image of him), and then to attribute to him nothing which is incongruent with immortality or incompatible with blessedness. Any view you hold about

αὐτοῦ δυνάμενον τὴν μετὰ ἀφθαρσίας μακαριότητα περὶ αὐτὸν δόξαζε. θεοὶ μὲν γὰρ εἰσίν· ἐναργὴς γὰρ αὐτῶν ἐστιν ἡ γνῶσις. οἵους δ᾽ αὐτοὺς ⟨οἱ⟩ πολλοὶ νομίζουσιν οὐκ εἰσίν· οὐ γὰρ φυλάττουσιν αὐτοὺς οἵους νομίζουσιν. ἀσεβὴς δὲ οὐχ ὁ τοὺς τῶν πολλῶν θεοὺς ἀναιρῶν, ἀλλ᾽ ὁ τὰς τῶν

God must be potentially consistent with these twin attributes of blessedness and immortality.

The existence of the gods is proved by the vividness of our knowledge of them. But people have inconsistent – and so invariably mistaken – ideas about what they're like. It isn't the attempt to refute the gods of popular belief which is a sign of irreligion; it's attributing to

πολλῶν δόξας θεοῖς προσάπτων. οὐ γὰρ προλήψεις εἰσὶν ἀλλ᾽ ὑπολήψεις ψευδεῖς αἱ τῶν πολλῶν ὑπὲρ θεῶν ἀποφάσεις· ἔνθεν αἱ μέγισται βλάβαι αἱ ἐπὶ τοῖς κακοῖς ἐκ θεῶν ἐπάγονται καὶ ὠφέλειαι. ταῖς γὰρ ἰδίαις οἰκειούμενοι διὰ παντὸς ἀρεταῖς τοὺς ὁμοίους ἀποδέχονται, πᾶν

the gods the qualities popularly attributed to them, because the usual notions about the gods rely on false suppositions rather than on empirical conceptions. This is the sense in which the gods are the source not just of exceptional benefits, but also of the terrible adversities which afflict bad people; it's the same principle as the one which makes people so thoroughly accustomed to their own good points that they accept others who resemble them-

τὸ μὴ τοιοῦτον ὡς ἀλλότριον νομίζοντες.

συνέθιζε δὲ ἐν τῷ νομίζειν μηδὲν πρὸς ἡμᾶς
εἶναι τὸν θάνατον ἐπεὶ πᾶν ἀγαθὸν καὶ κακὸν
ἐν αἰσθήσει· στέρησις δέ ἐστιν αἰσθήσεως ὁ
θάνατος. ὅθεν γνῶσις ὀρθὴ τοῦ μηθὲν εἶναι πρὸς
ἡμᾶς τὸν θάνατον ἀπολαυστὸν ποιεῖ τὸ τῆς ζωῆς

selves and regard anything different as alien.

It's very important to get into the habit of thinking that death is nothing to us. The reason is that nothing can be 'good' or 'bad' unless sense-experience is involved, and death is the absence of sense-experience. Here, then, is a way to make life enjoyable, for all its im-permanence: appreciating that death is nothing to us.

θνητόν, οὐκ ἄπειρον προστιθεῖσα χρόνον, ἀλλὰ
τὸν τῆς ἀθανασίας ἀφελομένη πόθον. οὐθὲν γάρ
ἐστιν ἐν τῷ ζῆν δεινὸν τῷ κατειληφότι γνησίως
τὸ μηδὲν ὑπάρχειν ἐν τῷ μὴ ζῆν δεινόν. ὥστε
μάταιος ὁ λέγων δεδιέναι τὸν θάνατον οὐχ ὅτι

You won't gain a life that goes on for ever and ever, but you will lose the pain of longing for immortality. There's no reason, you see, why anyone who has firmly grasped the fact that there's nothing frightening in the absence of life should find anything frightening in life.

W hat nonsense it is to say that the frightening aspect of death is not that it *will* make us suffer

λυπήσει παρών, ἀλλ' ὅτι λυπεῖ μέλλων. ὃ γὰρ
παρὸν οὐκ ἐνοχλεῖ, προσδοκώμενον κενῶς λυπεῖ.
τὸ φρικωδέστατον οὖν τῶν κακῶν ὁ θάνατος
οὐθὲν πρὸς ἡμᾶς, ἐπειδήπερ ὅταν μὲν ἡμεῖς
ὦμεν, ὁ θάνατος οὐ πάρεστιν, ὅταν δὲ ὁ θάνατος
παρῇ, τόθ' ἡμεῖς οὐκ ἐσμέν. οὔτε οὖν πρὸς τοὺς
ζῶντάς ἐστιν οὔτε πρὸς τοὺς τετελευτηκότας,
ἐπειδήπερ περὶ οὓς μὲν οὐκ ἔστιν, οἳ δ' οὐκέτι

when it arrives, but that anticipating its arrival makes us suffer *now!* I mean, what's the point in getting upset at the prospect of something which isn't upsetting when it's there? So death, the ultimate horror, is nothing to us, because it coincides only with the time when we don't exist, not when we do exist. In short, death is nothing to the living and nothing to the dead either, because it doesn't affect the living and the dead no longer exist.

33

εἰσίν. ἀλλ᾽ οἱ πολλοὶ τὸν θάνατον ὁτὲ μὲν ὡς
μέγιστον τῶν κακῶν φεύγουσιν, ὁτὲ δὲ ὡς
ἀνάπαυσιν τῶν ἐν τῷ ζῆν ‹κακῶν αἱροῦνται. ὁ
δὲ σοφὸς οὔτε παραιτεῖται τὸ ζῆν› οὔτε
φοβεῖται τὸ μὴ ζῆν· οὔτε γὰρ αὐτῷ προσίσταται
τὸ ζῆν οὔτε δοξάζεται κακὸν εἶναί τι τὸ μὴ ζῆν.
ὥσπερ δὲ τὸ σιτίον οὐ τὸ πλεῖον πάντως ἀλλὰ
τὸ ἥδιστον αἱρεῖται, οὕτω καὶ χρόνον οὐ τὸν

The usual practice is to vacillate between trying to avoid death on the grounds that it is the worst possible evil and inclining towards it on the grounds that it releases one from the troubles of life. A wise man, however, neither rejects life nor fears death; he doesn't regard life as a burden or death as an evil. His attitude towards time is the same as his attitude towards food: he chooses the nicest food rather than simply the larger por-

μήκιστον ἀλλὰ τὸν ἥδιστον καρπίζεται. ὁ δὲ
παραγγέλλων τὸν μὲν νέον καλῶς ζῆν, τὸν δὲ
γέροντα καλῶς καταστρέφειν, εὐήθης ἐστὶν οὐ
μόνον διὰ τὸ τῆς ζωῆς ἀσπαστόν, ἀλλὰ καὶ διὰ
τὸ τὴν αὐτὴν εἶναι μελέτην τοῦ καλῶς ζῆν καὶ
τοῦ καλῶς ἀποθνήσκειν. πολὺ δὲ χείρων καὶ ὁ

tion, and he relishes a pleasant life rather than merely a long one.

It's been suggested that while a young man should live well, an old man should die well. This is idiotic. In the first place, life is to be welcomed, and in the second place what you have to do to die well is the same as what you have to do to live well. But it's far worse for someone

λέγων ''καλὸν μὲν μὴ φῦναι, φύντα δ' ὅπως
ὤκιστα πύλας 'Αίδαο περῆσαι.'' εἰ μὲν γὰρ
πεποιθὼς τοῦτό φησιν, πῶς οὐκ ἀπέρχεται ἐκ
τοῦ ζῆν; ἐν ἑτοίμῳ γὰρ αὐτῷ τοῦτ' ἐστίν, εἴπερ
ἦν βεβουλευμένον αὐτῷ βεβαίως· εἰ δὲ μωκώμενος,
μάταιος ἐν τοῖς οὐκ ἐπιδεχομένοις. μνημονευτέον

to repeat Theognis' lines: 'It's a blessing not to be born; once born, however, it's a blessing to pass as quickly as possible through the gates of death.' If he's convinced of the truth of this, why doesn't he take his leave of life? The means are readily available, if he's really made up his mind; but if he's not serious, he's just mouthing empty words and no one will take the slightest notice of him. It's helpful to remember that although the future

δὲ ὡς τὸ μέλλον οὔτε ἡμέτερον οὔτε πάντως οὐχ ἡμέτερον, ἵνα μήτε πάντως προσμένωμεν ὡς ἐσόμενον μήτε ἀπελπίζωμεν ὡς πάντως οὐκ ἐσόμενον.

ἀναλογιστέον δὲ ὡς τῶν ἐπιθυμιῶν αἱ μέν εἰσι φυσικαί, αἱ δὲ κεναί. καὶ τῶν φυσικῶν αἱ μὲν ἀναγκαῖαι, αἱ δὲ φυσικαὶ μόνον· τῶν δ᾽

isn't ours to command, it isn't entirely beyond our control either. So we shouldn't simply expect future events to happen or despair of them happening at all.

It's important to be clear about desire. It's true that some desires are natural and others are pointless, but not all our natural desires are necessary: some are only natural. And what are the necessary desires necessary

ἀναγκαίων αἱ μὲν πρὸς εὐδαιμονίαν εἰσὶν
ἀναγκαῖαι, αἱ δὲ πρὸς τὴν τοῦ σώματος
ἀοχλησίαν, αἱ δὲ πρὸς αὐτὸ τὸ ζῆν. τούτων γὰρ
ἀπλανὴς θεωρία πᾶσαν αἵρεσιν καὶ φυγὴν
ἐπανάγειν οἶδεν ἐπὶ τὴν τοῦ σώματος ὑγίειαν
καὶ τὴν τῆς ψυχῆς ἀταραξίαν, ἐπεὶ τοῦτο τοῦ
μακαρίως ζῆν ἐστι τέλος. τούτου γὰρ χάριν
πάντα πράττομεν, ὅπως μήτε ἀλγῶμεν μήτε

for? Some are necessary for happiness, others for pacifying the body, others for life itself. Steady observation of our various desires enables us to guide our decisions about what to do and what not to do so that on each occasion we enhance our physical welfare and keep our minds free of disquiet – and this is the objective which is proper to a life of happiness. After all, freedom from pain and anxiety is the goal of everything we do.

ταρβῶμεν· ὅταν δ' ἅπαξ τοῦτο περὶ ἡμᾶς
γένηται, λύεται πᾶς ὁ τῆς ψυχῆς χειμών, οὐκ
ἔχοντος τοῦ ζῴου βαδίζειν ὡς πρὸς ἐνδέον τι
καὶ ζητεῖν ἕτερον ᾧ τὸ τῆς ψυχῆς καὶ τοῦ
σώματος ἀγαθὸν συμπληρώσεται. τότε γὰρ
ἡδονῆς χρείαν ἔχομεν ὅταν ἐκ τοῦ μὴ παρεῖναι
τὴν ἡδονὴν ἀλγῶμεν· ⟨ὅταν δὲ μὴ ἀλγῶμεν,⟩
οὐκέτι τῆς ἡδονῆς δεόμεθα. καὶ διὰ τοῦτο τὴν

If we succeed in this, the storm winds of the mind immediately settle: there's nothing living beings like ourselves feel we're missing and therefore have to go after, and there's nothing external we have to track down to promote a good physical and mental state. After all, we only lack pleasure when we don't have it; not having it causes us pain; therefore the end of pain is simultaneously the end of lacking pleasure.

ἡδονὴν ἀρχὴν καὶ τέλος λέγομεν εἶναι τοῦ μακαρίως ζῆν· ταύτην γὰρ ἀγαθὸν πρῶτον καὶ συγγενικὸν ἔγνωμεν, καὶ ἀπὸ ταύτης καταρχόμεθα πάσης αἱρέσεως καὶ φυγῆς καὶ ἐπὶ ταύτην καταντῶμεν ὡς κανόνι τῷ πάθει πᾶν ἀγαθὸν

Now you can appreciate why we call pleasure the beginning and end of a life of happiness. We've recognized that pleasure is our primary and innate good. We make it our starting-point in deciding what to do and what not to do, and we come back to it every time we refer to the feeling to assess the goodness of anything.

κρίνοντες. καὶ ἐπεὶ πρῶτον ἀγαθὸν τοῦτο καὶ σύμφυτον, διὰ τοῦτο καὶ οὐ πᾶσαν ἡδονὴν αἱρούμεθα, ἀλλ' ἔστιν ὅτε πολλὰς ἡδονὰς ὑπερβαίνομεν, ὅταν πλεῖον ἡμῖν τὸ δυσχερὲς ἐκ τούτων ἕπηται· καὶ πολλὰς ἀλγηδόνας ἡδονῶν κρείττους νομίζομεν, ἐπειδὰν μείζων ἡμῖν ἡδονὴ παρακολουθῇ πολὺν χρόνον ὑπομείνασι τὰς

The fact that pleasure is our primary and innate good also explains why we don't just go for all pleasures indiscriminately. There are occasions when intense pleasure *now* would cause an even greater degree of distress *later*, so we steer clear of it. And it's not at all uncommon for pain endured now to result later in pleasure which lasts for a long time and is more intense than the pain was: under these circumstances,

❧ 49 ❧

ἀλγηδόνας. πᾶσα οὖν ἡδονὴ διὰ τὸ φύσιν ἔχειν οἰκείαν ἀγαθόν, οὐ πᾶσα μέντοι αἱρετή· καθάπερ καὶ ἀλγηδὼν πᾶσα κακόν, οὐ πᾶσα δὲ ἀεὶ φευκτὴ πεφυκυῖα. τῇ μέντοι συμμετρήσει καὶ συμφερόντων καὶ ἀσυμφόρων βλέψει ταῦτα πάντα κρίνειν καθήκει· χρώμεθα γὰρ τῷ μὲν ἀγαθῷ κατά τινας

then, we prefer pain to pleasure. In other words, the fact that every pleasure is good, because it's naturally congenial to us, doesn't mean that every pleasure is worth going for. By the same token, just because every pain is bad, it doesn't follow that every pain always has to be avoided. The proper way to proceed is to assess every situation by weighing and surveying the advantages and disadvantages, because under certain conditions we

χρόνους ὡς κακῷ, τῷ δὲ κακῷ τοὔμπαλιν ὡς
ἀγαθῷ. καὶ τὴν αὐτάρκειαν δὲ ἀγαθὸν μέγα
νομίζομεν, οὐχ ἵνα πάντως τοῖς ὀλίγοις
χρώμεθα, ἀλλ᾽ ὅπως ἐὰν μὴ ἔχωμεν τὰ πολλά,
τοῖς ὀλίγοις χρώμεθα, πεπεισμένοι γνησίως ὅτι
ἥδιστα πολυτελείας ἀπολαύουσιν οἱ ἥκιστα

treat what is good as bad, and conversely what is bad as good.

Self-sufficiency also ranks high in our list of good qualities. The point is not to make do with little under all circumstances, but to do so if we don't have a lot. We're firmly convinced that it's those who have the least need of luxury who derive the greatest pleasure

ταύτης δεόμενοι, καὶ ὅτι τὸ μὲν φυσικὸν πᾶν
εὐπόριστόν ἐστι, τὸ δὲ κενὸν δυσπόριστον. οἵ
τε λιτοὶ χυλοὶ ἴσην πολυτελεῖ διαίτῃ τὴν ἡδονὴν
ἐπιφέρουσιν ὅταν ἅπαν τὸ ἀλγοῦν κατ' ἔνδειαν
ἐξαιρεθῇ· καὶ μᾶζα καὶ ὕδωρ τὴν ἀκροτάτην
ἀποδίδωσιν ἡδονὴν ἐπειδὰν ἐνδέων τις αὐτὰ
προσενέγκηται. τὸ συνεθίζειν οὖν ἐν ταῖς
ἁπλαῖς καὶ οὐ πολυτελέσι διαίταις καὶ ὑγιείας
ἐστὶ συμπληρωτικὸν καὶ πρὸς τὰς ἀναγκαίας

from it, and that while natural things are always easy to come by, it takes effort to supply oneself with things we don't really need. Plain fare affords as much pleasure as an extravagant diet as long as it gets rid of all the pain of need; bread and water are the most intensely enjoyable things in the world when they're served to someone who needs them. In short, the habit of a simple, inextravagant diet promotes health, makes a person face

τοῦ βίου χρήσεις ἄοκνον ποιεῖ τὸν ἄνθρωπον καὶ
τοῖς πολυτελέσιν ἐκ διαλειμμάτων προσερχομένους
κρεῖττον ἡμᾶς διατίθησι καὶ πρὸς τὴν τύχην
ἀφόβους παρασκευάζει. ὅταν οὖν λέγωμεν
ἡδονὴν τέλος ὑπάρχειν, οὐ τὰς τῶν ἀσώτων
ἡδονὰς καὶ τὰς ἐν ἀπολαύσει κειμένας λέγομεν,

the necessary business of life in a positive frame of mind, improves the way we deal with luxuries when they *do* appear from time to time, and enables us to face the vagaries of fortune without fear.

So when we say that pleasure is the goal of life, we're not talking about dissolute pleasures and we don't mean the pleasures of sensual indulgence either. This

ὥς τινες ἀγνοοῦντες καὶ οὐχ ὁμολογοῦντες ἢ κακῶς ἐκδεχόμενοι νομίζουσιν, ἀλλὰ τὸ μήτε ἀλγεῖν κατὰ σῶμα μήτε ταράττεσθαι κατὰ ψυχήν. οὐ γὰρ πότοι καὶ κῶμοι συνείροντες οὐδ' ἀπολαύσεις παίδων καὶ γυναικῶν οὐδ' ἰχθύων καὶ τῶν ἄλλων ὅσα φέρει πολυτελὴς τράπεζα τὸν ἡδὺν γεννᾷ βίον, ἀλλὰ νήφων λογισμὸς καὶ τὰς

view of our doctrine is due to ignorant contrariness or malicious misinterpretation. No, we're talking about freedom from physical discomfort and mental disquiet. A life of pleasure isn't the result of constant drinking and partying or the enjoyment of boys' and women's sexual favours or the consumption of fish and whatever else an extravagant table has to offer; a life of pleasure is the result of sober reasoning. Why? Because sober reasoning

αἰτίας ἐξερευνῶν πάσης αἱρέσεως καὶ φυγῆς καὶ τὰς δόξας ἐξελαύνων ἐξ ὧν πλεῖστος τὰς ψυχὰς καταλαμβάνει θόρυβος. τούτων δὲ πάντων ἀρχὴ καὶ τὸ μέγιστον ἀγαθὸν φρόνησις· διὸ καὶ φιλοσοφίας τιμιώτερον ὑπάρχει φρόνησις, ἐξ ἧς

enables you to examine your motives every time you decide what to do and what not to do, and to banish from your mind the ideas which cause people so much mental disquiet.

Now, this takes intelligence, and so intelligence heads our list of good qualities. In this sense, intelligence is more valuable even than philosophy. All the

αἱ λοιπαὶ πᾶσαι πεφύκασιν ἀρεταί, διδάσκουσα ὡς οὐκ ἔστιν ἡδέως ζῆν ἄνευ τοῦ φρονίμως καὶ καλῶς καὶ δικαίως, ‹οὐδὲ φρονίμως καὶ καλῶς καὶ δικαίως› ἄνευ τοῦ ἡδέως· συμπεφύκασι γὰρ αἱ ἀρεταὶ τῷ ζῆν ἡδέως, καὶ τὸ ζῆν ἡδέως τούτων ἐστὶν ἀχώριστον.

*other virtues depend on it. It shows that a life without in-
telligence, decency and morality is not a pleasant life,
and that a life without pleasure is not an intelligent,
decent and moral life, because the virtues are natural
adjuncts of a life of pleasure, and a life of pleasure is in-
separable from them.*

ἐπεὶ τίνα νομίζεις εἶναι κρείττονα τοῦ καὶ περὶ
θεῶν ὅσια δοξάζοντος καὶ περὶ θανάτου διὰ
παντὸς ἀφόβως ἔχοντος καὶ τὸ τῆς φύσεως
ἐπιλελογισμένου τέλος, καὶ τὸ μὲν τῶν ἀγαθῶν
πέρας ὡς ἔστιν εὐσυμπλήρωτόν τε καὶ εὐπόριστον
διαλαμβάνοντος, τὸ δὲ τῶν κακῶν ὡς ἢ χρόνους
ἢ πόνους ἔχει βραχεῖς, τὴν δὲ ὑπό τινων
δεσπότιν εἰσαγομένην πάντων ἂν γελῶντος

I submit, then, that the human ideal is to hold views about the gods which aren't sacrilegious, to be entirely without fear of death, and to have seen what the natural goal of life is. Such a person understands how easy it is to promote and gain the ultimate in goodness and how restricted either the duration or the intensity of badness is. He is able to scoff at fate (which some people suggest controls everything in the world) and to realize

‹εἱμαρμένην, ἀλλ᾽ ἃ μὲν κατ᾽ ἀνάγκην ὄντα συνορῶντος›, ἃ δὲ ἀπὸ τύχης, ἃ δὲ παρ᾽ ἡμᾶς, διὰ τὸ τὴν μὲν ἀνάγκην ἀνυπεύθυνον εἶναι, τὴν δὲ τύχην ἄστατον ὁρᾶν, τὸ δὲ παρ᾽ ἡμᾶς ἀδέσποτον ᾧ καὶ τὸ μεμπτὸν καὶ τὸ ἐναντίον παρακολουθεῖν πέφυκεν (ἐπεὶ κρεῖττον ἦν τῷ περὶ θεῶν μύθῳ κατακολουθεῖν ἢ τῇ τῶν φυσικῶν εἱμαρμένῃ δουλεύειν· ὁ μὲν γὰρ ἐλπίδα

instead that events may be due either to necessity or to fortune or to ourselves, because he appreciates that while necessity is beyond human control and fortune is evidently unstable, yet within our own sphere of responsibility we're subject to no external controlling forces and our actions are liable to praise or blame. In fact, it would be better to accept the stories about the gods than to enslave oneself to scientific determinism; at least the stories offer

παραιτήσεως ὑπογράφει θεῶν διὰ τιμῆς, ἡ δὲ
ἀπαραίτητον ἔχει τὴν ἀνάγκην), τὴν δὲ τύχην
οὔτε θεόν, ὡς οἱ πολλοὶ νομίζουσιν, ὑπολαμβάνοντος
(οὐθὲν γὰρ ἀτάκτως θεῷ πράττεται) οὔτε
ἀβέβαιον αἰτίαν (‹οὐκ› οἴεται μὲν γὰρ ἀγαθὸν

the faint hope that the gods might be induced by worship to change their minds, but scientific determinism recognizes only inexorable necessity.

As for fortune, he doesn't elevate it to divine status, as people commonly do — there's nothing chaotic about God's actions. Nor, on the other hand, does he take fortune to be an unreliable cause; he doesn't think it makes

ἢ κακὸν ἐκ ταύτης πρὸς τὸ μακαρίως ζῆν ἀνθρώποις δίδοσθαι, ἀρχὰς μέντοι μεγάλων ἀγαθῶν ἢ κακῶν ὑπὸ ταύτης χορηγεῖσθαι), κρεῖττον εἶναι νομίζοντος εὐλογίστως ἀτυχεῖν ἢ ἀλογίστως εὐτυχεῖν· βέλτιον γὰρ ἐν ταῖς πράξεσι τὸ καλῶς κριθὲν ‹μὴ ὀρθωθῆναι ἢ τὸ μὴ καλῶς κριθὲν› ὀρθωθῆναι διὰ ταύτην.

any kind of contribution, either good or bad, towards the happiness of human life, although he acknowledges that it supplies us with *opportunities* to enhance or worsen our lives significantly. He prefers to experience misfortune while acting rationally than to experience good fortune while acting irrationally, on the grounds that it's better for fortune to thwart the successful outcome of a good decision than to assist the successful outcome of a bad one.

ταῦτα οὖν καὶ τὰ τούτοις συγγενῆ μελέτα πρὸς
σεαυτὸν ἡμέρας, καὶ νυκτὸς πρὸς τὸν ὅμοιον
σεαυτῷ, καὶ οὐδέποτε οὔθ᾽ ὕπαρ οὔτ᾽ ὄναρ
διαταραχθήσῃ, ζήσῃ δὲ ὡς θεὸς ἐν ἀνθρώποις.
οὐθὲν γὰρ ἔοικε θνητῷ ζώῳ ζῶν ἄνθρωπος ἐν
ἀθανάτοις ἀγαθοῖς.

I urge you, then, to put these and compatible ideas into practice. Apply them to yourself in the daytime, and at night to anyone who reminds you of yourself; and then, whether you're awake or dreaming, you'll never be troubled by disquiet. Instead, you'll live as a god among men, because a person whose life is filled with divine blessings bears no resemblance to a human being.

EPICURUS' LIFE

Epicurus was born in 341 B.C., just a few years after the death of the ancient world's most famous philosopher, Plato. Like Plato, he came from an Athenian family, but his family had moved to the island of Samos (off the modern Turkish coast) not long before he was born. His father Neocles was a schoolteacher.

An early interest in philosophy was fostered by returning to Athens in 323 for military service. This gave young Epicurus the opportunity to study in the Academy (the school

founded by Plato) under Xenocrates; he would undoubtedly also have heard Aristotelian teachers in Athens. By now his family was living in Colophon, a town in Asia Minor north-east of Samos; after returning from Athens, Epicurus studied in nearby Teos under the Atomist philosopher Nausiphanes.

The next we hear of him is in 311, by which time he is acquiring a reputation as a teacher of his own brand of philosophy. A few years later he returned to Athens, where he settled and bought a house with a garden which formed the site of his school and gave it

its name – the Garden. Here he and a number of his followers lived communally and tried to put into practice Epicurus' precepts about living simply, quietly and apolitically, in order to attain the ideal of an untroubled mind, free from turmoil and disquiet. Unusually for the time, several women (some of whom had been prostitutes) were prominent among his disciples, and slaves or former slaves were also capable of joining. The community was not organized along democratic lines: Epicurus occupied the pinnacle as a kind of guru, and was revered by his devoted disciples, who were divided into several ranks. Epicurus died in 271 B.C.

He was a prolific writer, although very little of his work has survived. We know of the titles of a large number of books, on a large number of subjects. All that survives, however, are three letters and a couple of collections of brief precepts and maxims. Reconstructing the details of his philosophy depends largely on interpreting the works of later writers who were influenced by him: chief among these is the Latin poet Lucretius (94-55 B.C.). We know, then, that he had a strong theoretical interest in natural philosophy, and that in this sphere he inherited from the pre-Socratic philosophers Leucippus and Democritus (via Nausi-

phanes) the view that the ultimate constituents of the universe were indivisible particles called 'atoms'. He elaborated atomic physics until it could consistently account for the origin and nature of everything in the universe, large and small. He also made particular advances in developing atomism until it accounted for mental and psychological phenomena, such as sense-perception, dreams and even belief in the gods.

However, as his life in the Garden demonstrates, philosophy for Epicurus was above all a practical activity – a means of

perfecting oneself and freeing oneself from the anxieties to which we are normally prone. As a materialist, who believed that our perceptions and impressions are reliable, he naturally regarded our feelings of pleasure and pain as reliable criteria by which to judge the value of an action or event. Although it is absolutely clear that he never advocated sensual hedonism, this slur quickly became attached to him and his school by its superficial detractors — who were perhaps suspicious about exactly what the community members got up to in their secluded existence behind the walls of the Garden. In fact, he taught that intense physical pleasure is inevit-

ably bound up with intense pain; the only pleasures worth pursuing are those where the pleasant component outweighs the painful component — and these are few, and turn out to involve a life of quiet moderation. We should reduce our physical needs to promote freedom from physical discomfort and mental disquiet, and also rid ourselves of any practices or ideas (even commonly accepted ones) which might tend to worry us. The use of the term 'Epicurean' in the English language to mean 'out-and-out hedonist' is, then, both unfortunate and mistaken.